MY SCOTLAND

MY SCOTLAND

Hamish MacInnes

Constable · London

First published in Great Britain 1988
by Constable and Company Limited
10 Orange Street London WC2H 7EG

Set in Monophoto Photina 11pt by
BAS Printers Limited, Over Wallop, Hampshire
Printed and bound in Great Britain by
Richard Clay Limited, Bungay, Suffolk

British Library CIP data
My Scotland
1. Scotland
I. Title
941.1085'8

ISBN 0 09 467700 X

ACKNOWLEDGEMENTS

My thanks to all the people who helped me with this book; Libby Whittome who checked the manuscript; and especially Graeme Hunter whose expert advice on colour reproduction was invaluable. Also I am indebted to the Olympus Optical Company of Japan for the use of certain lenses.

H.M.I.
1988

INTRODUCTION

When one is as enthusiastic about Scotland as I am, there comes a desire to share with others, even if only through the lens of a camera, the beauty of its landscape, the magic of soft Highland lighting, and the seemingly limitless subtlety of its colours.

My work – writing, mountaineering and making films – has taken me into the remotest corners of Scotland. This book contains my own personal choice from a vast panorama, though I am aware that many other aspects of Scotland are equally fascinating. These photographs, though inevitably they fall short of reality, may, I hope, stir the reader to go and see for himself. The west coast, is, in my opinion, unequalled in scenic beauty; overflowing in history, spacious – yet remarkably accessible. The Western Highlands also feature prominently because this area is my favourite haunt; it is a region fragmented by sea and loch where a profusion of mountains provides a backcloth of rugged permanence founded on some of the oldest rock in the world.

This part of Scotland was at one time swathed in the great forest of Caledon and even today pockets of elegant Caledonian pines are still found in isolated groups. In the dim and distant past Mesolithic people and the flint-users from Ireland moved northwards; they were most likely succeeded by Neolithic tribes who built the chambered cairns that can still be seen, people of the sea who came up the west coast from the Mediterranean. Much later, in the Iron Age, vitrified forts were constructed, as well as brochs which are found only in the west and north of Scotland.

The Picts made an appearance here towards the end of the third century AD. They had the odd set-to with the Romans who also ventured north into this alien land, and so persistent was this harassment by the Picts that the Romans moved south to the Forth-Clyde boundary (the Antonine Wall) then later retreated yet further to Hadrian's Wall on the Scottish-English border.

In the early sixth century Scots came to this part of the country in increasing numbers, bringing Christianity with them. Notable amongst them was Columba, who in 563 founded the Celtic church. The inevitable disputes between Picts and Scots developed into a great struggle, with the Scots eventually emerging victorious; in 843 Kenneth MacAlpin became the first king of Scotland.

Next to dominate the western seaboard were the Vikings; they prevailed for four centuries and were not finally defeated till the Battle of Largs in 1263. Robert the Bruce, that veritable superman, came and went like a meteor through the War of Independence against the English, after seizing the Scottish throne in 1306. The clan system (where men bearing the same surname united under a clan chief) had evolved much earlier, but now, during an anarchic period in the Western Highlands, many clans merged for their own protection, several coming under the MacDonald umbrella, the MacDonald supremo assuming the title 'Lord of the Isles' about the year 1354.

An episode of major historical importance for Scotland, and one of the most famous in her history, took place in the Western Highlands: The Raising of the Standard at Glen Finnan in 1745. This marked the start of the Rising that attempted to put Prince Charles Edward Stuart on the Scottish throne. He first landed with his retinue on the Hebridean island of Eriskay on 23 July, and from there made his way to Glen Finnan in west Inverness-shire, but the adventure had sad and far-reaching effects on the Gaelic-speaking people of the Highlands, for after his rout at Culloden, England imposed its iron fist: the wearing of Highland dress was banned and the penalty for simply playing the pipes was transportation. Persecution was followed by famines between 1768 and 1773, when cattle died in their hundreds and crops failed. Emigration increased. The chiefs, instead of leading their clansmen in battle, became property owners and leased the lands to those with money. By the late 1700s it was realized that the coat of the sheep adequately protected it in Scotland's somewhat harsh environment, and this (as well as economic factors) heralded the beginning of the Clearances. People were evicted from their homes, driven to the harsh coastline and told to 'fish or die' – all to make way for the lairds' new four-legged friends. The clergy did little to help the people, and those who didn't leave for 'New Worlds' lived in hovels with no security of tenure. The lairds were also the magistrates and they held the Church in their pockets.

The turning point came at Braes in Skye when the womenfolk forced police to burn eviction orders. Two magistrates and sixty policemen returned and a battle, fought with sticks and stones, ensued. The police retreated to Portree, and William Gladstone, then Prime Minister, sent warships and troops to the islands to subdue the rebellious natives. The locals ignored them and went about their daily toil, and the Government finally got the message. The Crofters' Holding Act of 1886 was the result; amongst other concessions, it gave the crofter security of tenure.

This, then, is a brief synopsis of the history of this rugged countryside. Nowadays it remains a hill-farming region, dissected by large tracts of both conifer and deer forest, and everywhere tourism plays an increasing role in the rural economy.

Though *My Scotland* starts just north of the Firth of Clyde, there are other regions to the south which I was tempted to include, but it is the Highlands of Scotland which has for me the strongest appeal. The weather also plays a major role on this exposed landmass, but it is often the mist clinging to the slopes or shrouding the glens which gives it that special quality, not necessarily picture postcard days which can often for the photographer, be sterile.

Heading north on the A82 from Glasgow, one has a first taste of the Scottish Highlands in that unique combination of loch and ben by the 'bonnie banks' of Loch Lomond. Despite its proximity to Scotland's largest city, Loch Lomond, which is Britain's greatest expanse of fresh water, has undeniable charm. The song 'The Bonnie Banks of Loch Lomond' was written one evening by a prisoner held in Carlisle gaol who was to be executed the following morning for his part in the 1745 Rebellion. The lines 'You take the high road and I'll take the low road' do not refer to the present two roads: the 'high road' in the ballad means the way home; the 'low road', the route of the dead.

Loch Lomond has many historical connections. Rob Roy MacGregor, a Robin Hood-type reiver or rustler, lived here and a cave just north of Inversnaid on the eastern shore still bears his name. But Robert the Bruce used this cave in 1306 long before Rob Roy's debut on the Highland stage. The old fort at Inversnaid was sacked twice by the MacGregor clan and was later under the command of General Wolfe (of Quebec siege fame), then a young officer.

The Cobbler (881m, 2891ft) can be seen from Tarbet on Loch Lomondside, a jagged mountain comprising three separate peaks. The Centre Peak is the highest and its two companions are the South Peak, sometimes called Jean (the Cobbler's wife) and the North Peak. The mountain's official name is Ben Arthur, but it is never called that nowadays. It consists of mica schist and is popular with Glaswegian rock-climbers.

Mull has a particular attraction which is difficult to define. Parts of it are wild and Highland-like, other areas are pastoral and secluded. Being an island certainly adds to its feeling of remoteness and charm, yet it is easily accessible from Oban or from Lochaline in Morvern. Tobermory is the principal town on the island, really a glorified village clustered around a perfect bay and harbour. Here, in November 1588, the *San Juan de Sicilia*, a galleon of the Spanish Armada, blew up, reputedly with treasure aboard. All attempts to recover the treasure have failed, and it is doubtful whether indeed there ever was treasure aboard. I think my favourite corner of Mull is the south coast at the Carsaig Arches, where a fine walk along the shore from Loch Buie takes one past the Nuns' Cave. Iona and Staffa can be visited from Oban on a day trip, though this somewhat limits one's sightseeing capabilities on Mull. Iona, this cradle of Christianity, has had a profound effect on Scotland. St Columba was its most famous saint – a poacher turned gamekeeper, since before his landfall on Scottish soil he was responsible for the great Battle of Cooldrevny in Ireland in which thousands perished. Vowing that he would not return to his native Ireland until he had gained for Christ a number of souls equal to those lost in the battle, he landed at Port na Curaichon on Iona on 12 May 563, when he was forty-two years old. Iona, as well as being called the Cradle of Christianity, is sometimes also known as Blessed Iona or Jewel of the Western Sea, and it is, even today, a place of pilgrimage for thousands of tourists. It is owned by the National Trust for Scotland. Iona's original name was the Norse 'I' which simply means 'island'.

Staffa is one of the Treshnish group of islands to the north of Iona. Its name, meaning 'Isle of Staves' in Norse, derived from the unique columnar basalt rock which characterizes it. It is, of course, famed for Fingal's Cave, immortalized by Mendelssohn. However, the cave was associated with music even before the visit of that renowned composer, for its Gaelic name is Uamh Binne, the Musical Cave, which refers to the pounding of the waves inside it.

Awesome Glencoe seems to impart a feeling of history and emotional turmoil. Charles Dickens wrote of it when he visited Glencoe in 1842: 'The pass is an awful place. There are scores of glens higher up, which form such haunts as you might imagine yourself wandering in the very height of madness of a fever . . .' Despite Dickens's misgivings, I find the glen a wonderful place, always changing, a valley of many moods; fascinating whether in an autumnal deluge with white parallel torrents cascading down the dark face of Aonach Dubh; in the teeth of an Arctic blizzard; or in the astounding clarity of a fine spring day. People subject to claustrophobia find the glen oppressive, for it is narrow and deep like a slit trench, with the A82 highway furtively snaking along the valley floor; a good place for an ambush, a soldier might say. Indeed, as is well known, the Campbells made use of the physical characteristics of the area to perpetrate their dastardly deed on 13 February 1692. After being billeted for about a fortnight on the MacDonalds of Glencoe and accepting their hospitality, the Campbell soldiers set upon their hosts on the morning of the 13th and murdered forty souls, men, women and children. Many more succumbed to the icy blizzard in attempting to escape up side valleys. This deed of the Campbells', 'Murder under Trust', was the most heinous of Scottish crimes, carrying the quadruple penalties of hanging, disembowelling, beheading and quartering.

The motive for the Massacre can be found in the national pastime of the period, cattle-rustling or reiving. The MacDonalds were singled out as they were particularly adept at the sport and their lands bordered those of their powerful neighbours, the Campbells. The official reason for the action was that an oath of allegiance to the Crown had not been taken by MacIain, the MacDonald chief. (In fact, MacIain did sign, but for various reasons had delayed in doing so, which gave the enemies of the MacDonalds of Glencoe the opportunity they were waiting for.) Breadalbane and the Master of Stair had been hatching their plot to exterminate the Glencoe MacDonalds since early December, assuming the old chief would refuse to give allegiance. Dalrymple wrote to his co-conspirator: 'The winter is the only season in which we are sure the Highlanders cannot escape us, nor carry their wives, bairns and cattle to the mountains.'

Nowadays you are quite safe in the Glen, even if your name is Campbell – although at least one hotel, until quite recently, wouldn't knowingly accept guests from the Campbell clan, and the singer Glen Campbell was turned away from a local hostelry.

To the east of Glencoe is the fastness of the Moor of Rannoch, a desolate yet beautiful wilderness, at one time clothed in the Black Wood of Rannoch. Guides used to navigate travellers through its fifty-six-square-mile maze, but now the main road makes its way westwards across the Moor to Glencoe.

Glen Etive, as if frightened by Glencoe, shoots off to the south at Buachaille Etive Mor and nudges the head of Loch Etive some twelve miles down this scenic glen. It is lush in its lower reaches and has a compulsive attraction for the Highland midge, a creature with an insatiable appetite.

Fort William's main claim to fame is that it lies at

the foot of Ben Nevis, the highest mountain in Britain (1344m, 4408ft) and, one could also say, at the foot, or the westerly end, of the Great Glen and Caledonian Canal. The original Fort was constructed by General Monck in 1654 and no longer exists, but Inverlochy Castle is still extant, albeit weather- and battle-worn. The original structure is supposed to date from 1260, and even that was probably on the site of a much older fort. The present castle dates from the late fifteenth century. In 1645 the famous Battle of Inverlochy was fought close by, between Montrose and the Convenanting army under Campbell of Argyll; though outnumbered two to one, Montrose was victorious. His march to the Castle to engage Campbell's forces, prior to the battle, was an outstanding example of military strategy. A famous poet, Iain Lom, who accompanied Montrose, recorded in his memorable verse, 'The Day of Inverlochy':

> . . . Alasdair, noble son of Colla, right hand for cleaving the castles, you put the rout on the grey Saxons and if they drank kail-broth you emptied it out of them.

Like Oban, Fort William is an important tourist and shopping centre, with road and rail links to Mallaig. It is a stepping-stone to Skye and the Small Isles, Eigg, Rhum, Canna and Muck – enchanting names. It is also possible to reach by road from Fort William the most westerly place on the British mainland, Ardnamurchan Point (Point of the Great Ocean), which lies twenty-three miles west of Land's End. It is a backwater worth exploring, with wonderful beaches, and is probably even more dramatic in stormy weather. However, to return to Fort William, both Glen Nevis, which skirts the southerly slopes of Ben Nevis, and the Ben itself are worth mentioning. Upper Glen Nevis is a hanging valley to which you have to walk from the car-park and which is well worth the small effort. It is graced by the Steall Falls, and from it the summit of Ben Nevis can be seen. The Ben's most spectacular face is, however, on the north-east side and this can be viewed from the Great Glen road a few miles out of Fort William. It is a bad-weather mountain, being subject to severe winter blizzards, and even in summer snow can fall on the summit.

Westwards from Fort William the Mallaig road takes you through breathtaking scenery: mountain, loch, and glen are steeped in Scottish history. It was at Glen Finnan that the Standard was raised in 1745 in the ill-fated Jacobite Rebellion. Prince Charles Edward Stuart who led this uprising landed on the mainland at nearby Loch nan Uamh, a few miles beyond. After his defeat at the Battle of Culloden, he escaped the clutches of the Redcoats and eventually embarked on a French ship which returned him to France. He was later to die a drunken and disillusioned man.

Mallaig is a shadow of its former self as a fishing port, but is still a ferry point for the Isle of Skye and the gateway to Knoydart and the islands of Canna, Rhum, Muck and Eigg, places which should feature prominently on any tourist's itinerary.

Knoydart is accessible by boat from Mallaig, across the mouth of Loch Nevis, and its northern side can be reached from Kinlochhourn, at the head of Loch Hourn. No roads lead into Knoydart, but there are good paths offering superb walks. To the north of Knoydart is Kintail with Glenelg providing a centre from which to explore its scenic delights. From Glenelg the Kyle Rhea ferry plies to the 'Winged' Isle of Skye, access being from Kintail over the sinuous Mam Ratagan Pass. Glen Shiel and the A87 form the highway to Skye. It is a glen of shapely mountains, especially the five peaks on the right as you head north and west – the Five Sisters of Kintail. Legend has it that at one time there were seven daughters of the local chief, two of whom were taken off as brides by two brothers, both Irish fishermen. Upon their departure the Irishmen promised to return with their five brothers to claim the remaining sisters. Years passed with no sign of this amorous Irish invasion, so, to prevent the five patient sisters from fading with old age, the local medicine man turned them into these graceful mountains where, agelessly, they could look out over the loch and watch for the landfall of their overdue bridegrooms. We must selfishly hope that the wayward Irish gentlemen never materialize to rob us of these lovely petrified maidens.

Eilean Donan Castle seems to brood over its chequered past in splendid isolation at the meeting of three lochs in Kintail: Loch Alsh, Loch Duich and Loch Long. One of the seats of the Mackenzie clan, it was built seven hundred years ago on the site of an early vitrified fort, part of which can still be seen today. It changed hands several times over the centuries and in 1313 the Earl of Murray, obviously a bit of a showman, draped fifty of his enemies' heads from the curtain walls. The Castle was restored in 1932 at a cost of £250,000. Like Glencoe and Glen Torridon, Kintail is owned by the National Trust for Scotland, guardian of Scotland's natural treasures.

The Vikings called Skye 'Skuyo', the Cloud Island; this name many visitors may feel appropriate. Even today, one can still imagine the longships of the Norsemen turning the headlands to gain the shelter of one of its many sea lochs. The Vikings were here for three centuries and many of the place-names are Norse. It is a fascinating island with a particular magic about it; some people find it irresistible and spend the rest of their days here. Like most other places in the Western Highlands, it has more than its fair share of history, but it is the scenery itself which is so stunning.

The two main ranges of hills, the Black and Red Cuillin, dominate Skye; both are in the southern half of the island, the rest being less rugged, with the exception of Storr and the Quiraing. It is above all the coastline which offers the three-star views.

Skye is an island of forts; almost every prominent headland boasting a view has a ruined fort or dun. Its castles, too, are worth visiting, the most famous being Dunvegan which houses the Bratach Sith, the Fairy Flag of the MacLeods. This is reputed to have been a consecrated banner of the Knights Templar, captured from the Saracens during the Crusades. The story goes that it was presented to William, the fourth chief of the MacLeods, by his fairy (the old meaning of the word) lover and should only be displayed in three types of emergency: when the sole heir is in danger of death; when the clan is being defeated; or when the clan faces extinction. To date it has been unfurled twice in battle, whereupon the hard-pressed MacLeods emerged victorious.

At the north end of Skye in Trotternish are the ruins of Duntulm Castle, originally the site of Dun Dabhaid, the fortress home of Biornal, a Norse princess. Duntulm was also for many years a MacLeod possession, one of whose chiefs, Donald Gorm, after being killed whilst leading a siege of Eilean Donan Castle, returned to haunt Duntulm. As he was partial to wine, a legacy of the 'Auld Alliance' with France, his hauntings were of an inebriated nature and he also insisted on having noisy 'spiritual' friends at these 'parties'.

Portree is the principal town on the Isle of Skye. It derived its name from the Gaelic, 'Port a Righ', the King's Port, following a diplomatic visit by King James V in 1540 when he was trying to pacify the troublesome Western Isles. It was here, too, that the fleeing Prince Charlie bade farewell to Flora MacDonald: romantic traditionalists would have us see it as a touching parting, but more reliable sources cast doubt on this.

The long chain of islands to the west of the Scottish mainland, like a matured Barrier Reef, known as the Outer Hebrides, still seems to have one foot in the past. Even today Gaelic is the first language of these islanders, where, as on the Isle of Skye, time appears to freewheel. If you do not have to hurry it is a place to visit, especially in spring.

Beyond, in the wide Atlantic, one hundred and ten miles from the mainland, is St Kilda, a windswept archipelago which is home for a multitude of seabirds, a few military personnel and the occasional, resolute, seasick visitor. In 1930 the indigenous human population of St Kilda was evacuated to the mainland owing to crop failure and lack of medical facilities; thus ended a unique society where everything was shared. There was even a 'Queen' of St Kilda. Birds rather than fish were the staple diet of these hardy people; in the late 1800s, 89,000 puffins were killed and dried each year. One can only conclude that the St Kildans had voracious appetites, for gannets and fulmars were consumed in even greater numbers.

Back on terra firma, the ragged coastline of Scotland continues northwards from the Kyle of Lochalsh in a profusion of sea lochs and headlands. For a while at least the road, as it heads for Applecross and Torridon, diminishes to a winding single track punctuated by laybys, reminiscent of a snake corpulent with undigested meals.

We now enter an area of Old Torridonian Sandstone, where the tiered mountains of Applecross rear like haughty red castles. This is superb country, providing in winter some of the best snow- and ice-climbing in Scotland, and in summer delectable hill walks, the tops of all being within easy reach of the summit of Bealach na Ba, the Pass of the Cattle (625m, 2053ft) which takes you back over the mountains to the west coast and the snug white houses of Applecross.

From here the road northwards follows round the snout of the Applecross peninsula to hug the south shore of Loch Torridon. I have a soft spot for Torridon, considering it a home from home. On a good day few places on earth can compete with its abundant beauties. Everywhere there is space, and few fences or restraints keep you in your car. The road, the A896, now takes you up through Glen Torridon, with the prodigious mass of Liathach, the Grey One, on the left. A gap, Coire Dubh, between its shapely bulk and the next peak, Beinn Eighe, provides a gateway to the great northern corries of these mountains; superb walks justly reward those who make the effort.

At Kinlochewe, the road from Garve and Dingwall

comes in on the right whilst the A832 follows the side of Loch Maree, which is dominated by Slioch (980m, 3217ft) to the north. In the not too distant past a postman used to walk the nineteen-mile (30km) path, precipitous in places, on the north side of Loch Maree carrying mail to Poolewe for the Western Isles.

To the north of Loch Maree is some of the most remote and unspoiled country in the British Isles – long may it remain so. Though it is possible to walk through this region in a couple of days, to Carnmore then on to Dundonnell, the A832 takes the motorist more easily round the west end of Loch Maree to Gairloch and Inverewe Gardens, and up the coast to Dundonnell.

An Teallach is the mountain towering over Dundonnell. However, it is seen to best advantage some way beyond, where the road starts to climb towards Braemore Junction on the main Ullapool drag. An Teallach means 'The Forge' in Gaelic, and it is a unique mountain, the main peaks crowding round Toll an Lochain, a black mirror of a loch beneath the Torridonian Sandstone cliffs. This road was once called the Destitution Road, and was built originally as a single track, during the 1851 potato famine.

Ullapool could be described as fulfilling a similar function to Oban or Fort William: it is a popular tourist centre, and from it a ferry serves the Outer Hebrides. It is also a fishing port. During the mackerel season in the autumn a profusion of factory-ships anchor in Loch Broom, providing an amazing spectacle and served mainly by Scottish fishing-boats. These factory-ships, many from Eastern Europe and the Soviet Union, are called 'Klondikers', and during this period the town is thronged with Russian, East German and Polish sailors. Several local traders have now acquired a smattering of Russian.

From Ullapool the main road runs north into wild-west country, where side roads take you to places such as Achiltibuie and the 'back road' to Lochinver. However, for once it is the main highway, the A837, that is the most impressive way of approaching the quaint fishing village of Lochinver, where sheep are as common as pedestrians on its only street.

You are now in Sutherland, a name derived from the Vikings who called this area 'Sudrland', the South Land. To the east behind the village, completely dominating the moorland desert, is Suilven (731m, 2399ft), an enormous sandstone tombstone, capped, like many of the peaks in this much-forgotten quarter, with grey quartzite. But you will have already made acquaintance with this prodigious peak as you drove round it from the east – like a quick-changing model, it offers varied and enticing angles.

The A837 continues northwards from Loch Assynt, where that daring and innovative patriot Montrose was betrayed and captured. A bridge now replaces the services of the Kylesku Ferry. Here, too, the B869 comes in as an alternative route from Lochinver, a road which was until recently both tortuous and narrow, passing close to the sea stack known as the Old Man of Stoer (not to be confused with the Old Man of Storr on Skye).

You are now rapidly running out of land as you near Cape Wrath, passing through Reay Forest, which to non-Scots seems something of a misnomer, for trees here are as scarce as full whisky bottles. Such tracts of rock, mountain, moorland and peat frequented by deer are known hereabouts as 'deer forests'.

Scourie is the next village, an odd assortment of houses whose traditional, no-nonsense cottages still look as if they'll outlast the ticky-tacky newer ones. It is a centre for fisher people, hill-walkers and bird-watchers. With its galaxy of freshwater lochs, sea lochs and peaty lochans, one wonders if an Admiralty chart wouldn't be a better document by which to 'navigate'.

Just beyond the village is the turn-off for the tiny hamlet of Tarbet and the boat for the delights of Handa Island, though sometimes a boat is also available from Scourie. Tarbet has sad associations for me. When two colleagues and I made the first ascent of the Great Stack of Handa in 1972, a fisherman, Alasdair Munro took us to the base of the Great Stack in his small boat. Later that year he went missing whilst lobster fishing, and his body was later recovered from the Sound of Handa. Before this, in 1958, three other members of his family were drowned close to the island, and in 1974 another of his sons was swept overboard and drowned off Tiree.

Handa, one and half miles by one mile, has an enormous population for its size. A census in 1962 showed that there were a total of 90,800 . . . birds. This is a famous sea-bird sanctuary which comes under the aegis of the Royal Society for the Protection of Birds, and to visit it during the nesting season in May and June is to see a place of great wonder.

When I was taking the photograph in this book of the Great Stack, a French tourist was in a high state of excitement at seeing so huge a mass of razorbills crowding every impossible ledge, like an opera audience in dinner jackets. I tried to explain to him in my appalling French that the Stack was perched on five great sandstone legs, hidden except at the lowest of tides. By holding my five fingers downwards, I illustrated by gesture what I failed to impart in his language. At first he looked at me in amazement, then in disbelief. It was only upon the arrival of his English-speaking wife that the matter was clarified: 'My husband tells me that you explained to him that all the birds on Great Stack have five legs!'

Beyond the cluster of houses which bears the name Rhiconich, on an offshoot of the A838, is Kinlochbervie, a busy white-fish port with two separate jetties. This road ends at Sheigra, the last outpost on Scotland's west coast. Dotted along the sea-coast are some magnificent beaches, but by far the finest is Sandwood Bay, to which you have to walk from just beyond Oldshore More. This rivals any beach, anywhere. Great breakers roll in unimpeded to wash its vast expanse of sand, for there is no land between here and the North Pole. The ruins of a house, reputedly haunted, brood above the beach, and a short way inland is the freshwater Sandwood Loch.

Before returning southwards to the Cairngorms to see more of my Scottish gems, it is worth visiting the scalp of the Scottish mainland adjoining the often turbulent Pentland Firth. Here there are two fine mountains, Ben Hope and Ben Loyal, lonely sentinels in this far-flung corner of Scotland. From their summits you can, on a good day, look across the often stormy waters to the Island of Hoy and see the Old Man of Hoy, Britain's most impressive sea stack, with the enormous cliffs of St John's Head behind it. The two live television broadcasts which we did when climbing the stack brought this somewhat unstable pillar of Torridonian Sandstone into the living-rooms of millions of viewers.

The great mass of the Cairngorms in the Southern Highlands form the roof of Scotland, spreading from Aviemore in the north of the area to Blairgowrie in the south, and almost to Aberdeen in the east. This whole range of mountains, now generally known by its collective name, the Cairngorms, has a peculiar attraction, quite unlike that of the mountains of the west, since they are more rolling and not quite so colourful. Nevertheless, walking across the high Cairngorm plateau gives you the feeling that you are on top of the world. The Aviemore area is of course commercialized; skiing is the great winter attraction while in summer the visitor has the choice of many outdoor activities, with the bad-weather reserve of the hotel complexes and their in-house entertainments. However, with the exception of a few popular routes, most other areas in these mountains are deserted. They are places where you can get away from it all, and in the spring you can walk the tops and remoter glens for days without encountering a soul – a rare experience in today's Europe.

The most popular centres for mountaineers are the northern peaks near Aviemore, Lochnagar and Creagan Dhu Lochan, reached from Royal Deeside; to a lesser extent, Glen Doll and Glen Clova which has access from the south east, are also popular, especially with Dundonians.

This book can allow you only a glimpse of this fascinating land, but I trust that *My Scotland* may entice you to venture forth and explore and find 'your Scotland'.

[1] Ben Lomond from upper Loch Lomond.

[2] The Cobbler, which stands above Arrochar, Loch Long, has three summits: the South, the Centre (which is the highest) and the North.

[3] Oban, the gateway to the isles. Above the town is McCaig's Tower – a folly, some say, and a miniature of the Colosseum of Rome. It was built between 1890 and 1900 by John Stuart McCaig, an Oban banker, to provide work for the local unemployed.

[4] Carsaig Arches, Mull.

[5] The wonderful ruins of St Mary's, Iona, probably Scotland's most beautiful nunnery.

[6] Fingal's Cave, Island of Staffa. Staffa is Norse for Stave Island. The Vikings constructed the walls of their houses with vertical logs like these basaltic columns. A visit to the cave in 1829 inspired Mendelssohn to write his 'Hebrides' Overture.

TAFFA

[7] The summit of Ben Lui, near Tyndrum.

[8] Kingshouse Hotel, Glencoe is one of the oldest licensed inns in Scotland. It was an old drovers' stance, and is more comfortable today than when Dorothy Wordsworth visited it: 'The first thing we saw on entering the door was two sheep hung up, as if just killed from the barren moor, their bones hardly sheathed in flesh.'

[9] Buachaille Etive Mor, the eastern citadel of Glencoe. The Buachaille, as it is affectionately known to climbers, is one of the finest mountains in Britain and it is a Mecca for both the summer rock-climber and the winter mountaineer.

[10] A view northwards towards Glencoe from a small loch in Glen Etive.

[11] Buachaille Etive Mor, from under an old General Wade bridge near Altnafeadh. Coire na Tulaich, centre of picture, is the normal descent route off the mountain.

[12] Buachaille Etive Beag, Glencoe – the 'Small Herdsman' – in winter.

[13] Allt na ruigh cottage, Glencoe. Across the valley is Coire Gabhail, 'Corrie of the Plunder'. It was here that the MacDonalds of Glencoe hid stolen cattle. The three peaks which dominate the south side of the glen are Beinn Fhada, Gearr Aonach and Aonach Dubh.

[14] The Lost Valley, Glencoe, Coire Gabhail.

[15] Achnambeithach cottage and Loch Achtriochtan with Stob Coire nam Beith behind.

[16] From July until the end of September sheep are gathered and taken down to the fanks at Achtriochtan. They are seen here on the old road.

[17] The monarch of the glen with the Aonach Eagach Ridge behind.

[18] Aonach Dubh, the 'Black Ridge'.

[19] This Highland cow could easily be mistaken for a yak, and the setting for the Himalayas. Behind is the Fionn Ghleann which leads over to Glen Etive from the lower reaches of Glencoe.

[20] Red sails on Loch Leven, with the Pap of Glencoe behind.

[21] Fine winter conditions on the perfect horseshoe ridge of Beinn a'Bheithir above Ballachulish.

[22] A Druid standing stone at Onich, with the peaks of Glencoe.

[23] Scottish blue belles.

[24] Sunset at the old pier at Kentallen, with the hills of Ardgour beyond Loch Linnhe.

[25] Castle Stalker, Appin, dates back to the fifteenth century. It was built as a hunting-seat by Duncan Stuart for James IV, and saw 'battle' during the shooting of the Monty Python film, *The Holy Grail*.

[26] Tioram Castle, Moidart.

[27] Inverlochy Castle, Fort William: the original castle dates from 1260.

[28] Ben Nevis in its winter garment.

[29] Steall Waterfall, upper Glen Nevis.

[30] Ben Nevis from Corpach.

[31] The north-east face of Ben Nevis from near Gairlochy.

[32] The '45 memorial, Glen Finnan.

[33] The '45 memorial, Glen Finnan: it was here that the standard was raised for the 1745 Rebellion.

[34] Weekend rest, Mallaig harbour.

[35] The Sgurr of Eigg. The Cave of Francis on Eigg is where 395 MacDonalds were suffocated by the MacLeods of Skye.

[36] Lambs at play, and the Sgurr of Eigg.

[37] The monument of Torr a'Bhalbhain, Knoydart at the junction of the Gleann Meadail and Barrisdale paths.

[38] Loch Hourn, with Ladhar Bheinn in the distance.

[39] Salmon-fishing, Loch Duich, Kintail.

[40] Oil-seed rape is now a common crop in Scotland.

[41] Linseed: when it is in bloom, the delicate blue flowers are shed each day.

[42] Loch Long, Kintail.

[43] Looking back at the Five Sisters of Kintail from the road to Loch Carron.

[44] Casteal Maol, Kyleakin, Isle of Skye. According to legend, a Norse princess put a chain across the narrows to the mainland and extracted a toll from passing ships. Times haven't changed much: you still have to pay for the ferry!

[45] The Black Cuillin at sunset from Ord, Sleat, Isle of Skye.

[46] Blaven from Torren. This isolated part of the Cuillin of Skye has a magical appeal.

[47] The Cuillin from near Struan.

[48] The Cuillin from Elgol. Loch Coruisk is hidden in the great rock horseshoe of the Black Cuillin beyond the head of Loch Scavaig.

[49] The Pinnacle Ridge of Sgurr nan Gillean in winter.

[50] A golden eagle and chick in the Cuillin.

[51] The Cioch, Sron na Ciche. Cioch means Breast and it was first discovered and climbed by Professor Norman Collie. He first saw its shadow on the slab below.

[52] The cliffs of Rubha nan Clach from Ullinish.

[53] The Quiraing in north Skye. This is a view from the 'Table'. 'Quiraing' in Norse means the 'Pillared Cattle Pen'.

[54] Staffin Bay with Flodigarry in the background.

[55] Kilt Rock.

[56] The Old Man of Storr and two of his minions, with the island of South Rona.

[57] Peinchorran from across Loch Sligachan with the hills of Storr beyond.

[58] Castlebay, Barra with the MacNeill fortress, Kisimul Castle.

[59] The standing stones of Callernish, North Lewis, are next in importance to Stonehenge.

[60] St Kilda, the island of Hirta. Here a cleat is seen with Village Bay beyond. Cleats were used for air-drying seabirds; together with eggs, these were the staple diet of the St Kildans.

[61] Loch Kishorn with Beinn Bhan and the Cioch behind.

[62] Shieldaig village, and the rugged *gneiss* to the north of Loch Torridon.

[63] Loch a Ghlas-tuil on the north side of Liathach, a splendidly isolated lochan.

[64] Liathach, the 'Grey One', from Loch Clair, Torridon.

[65] Toll an Lochain, An Teallach.

[66] Loch Kanaird with Ben More Coignach.

[67] Stac Polly, Cul Mor and Cul Beag from Achnahaird.

[68] Highland dancing.

5
6
7
8
12

[69] Ardvreck Castle, Loch Assynt, with Quinag.

[70] Lochinver and Suilven.

[71] Sail Garbh, Quinag from near Kylesku.

[72] Sail Garbh, Quinag from Unapool.

[73] The Stack of Glencoul from Unapool.

[74] Badcoll Bay.

[75] The Great Stack of Handa.

[76] Handa Puffin.

[77] Oldshore Mor.

[78] Am Buachaill, Sandwood Bay.

[79] The Old Man of Hoy, Orkney, Britain's most spectacular sea stack.

[80] Whisky 'pagodas' – the malting houses at Drumochter distillery.

[81] Ruthven Barracks, Kingussie.

[82] The eighteenth-century Bridge of Carr, Carrbridge.